W9-DHY-069

La place de la Bourse à Bordeaux

L'Esprit d'un Terroir

A voyage of discovery through the vineyards of Bordeaux

Jean-Claude Berrouet

Gilles d'Auzac de Lamartinie

L'Esprit d'un Terroir

A voyage of discovery through the vineyards of Bordeaux

Translation : Fiona Morrison M.W.

Editions Premier Pas

The timeless regard of the winegrower recounts the long saga of vineyards and wine.
The widening steps to keep pace with the ox or the horse ploughing the long rows between the vines: the picnic snacks washed down with local wine at the end of a row of vines or next to the old wooden vats.....
This is the timelessness of wine, long before the Loi Evin!

In the libournais, an old hut covered by ivy reminds us that in the past, it sheltered the worker and his beast during his mealtimes or from a storm.

*W*hether pebbley or clayey, the wine must tell the tale of its native soil.
Bravo the gravel soils which produce scarlet sometimes crimson tinted wines with elegant and complex bouquets where rich balsamic aromas overlap with the vivacity of spices and the roundness of tobacco. These are classic, well structured wines, with solid tannins and a firm texture.
Bravo to the clay soils which produce purple hued wines with rich and intense aromas, where scents of truffle blend with bitter almonds and licorice. They coat the mouth like a velvet ball and awaken our senses. These are young seducers!

*I*n Moulis-en-Médoc, a pale wintry sun for the last time spotlights the trunks, stripped of their leaves.
Coloured burnt siena by the heat of the August sun, they wait to be pruned.

During the winter, the divested vine submits its woody skeleton to the shears of the secateur.
The skill of the pruner is to handle each vine according to its vigour and to prepare it for the future harvest.
The vine cuttings, once cleared away, have differing destinies. Here in Margaux, they are burnt on the spot.....elsewhere they are bundled and stored to light a fire at a later date on which a good steak will be grilled.

S*trolling through the labyrinthine lanes of Pomerol, a traveller can be surprised by the small scale of some of the estates. The vines brush up against the buildings, using up all of the available space to create an enchanted garden.*

The stakes without which the vine could not fall into line, previously made of aca-
cia, are today made of pine and gradually become worn with time.
During winter, the workers see to replacing them. One can hear the clear, staccato
echoes of hammering as the new stakes are driven into the unyielding soil.

$\mathcal{T}$hese old serried vines with twisted arms release their first leaves.
They reassure us; they are still alive and will once again produce wines worthy of
the appellation of the Côtes de Blaye.

In the region of Loupiac, a flourishing soil presents the first flowers of spring to a century old vine.
Will the vine remember them by yielding some floral aromas during the next harvest?

$\mathcal{S}$killed, confident, intelligent hands needed to retighten wires, bundle together vine cuttings, prune the new wood, squeeze a berry to see how its pulp is ripening, cover a barrel's bung with freshly cut rushes or to knead the pomace to ensure that it has drained well.

$\mathcal{T}$aking the little winding roads of Sainte-Croixe-du-Mont, the traveller discovers a landscape of a forgotten time.
An ancient worn out press finds a new youth as it surrounds a blossoming tree.

*O*n an April morning, *"Rêveuse", the last mare working in the vineyards of Saint Emilion, pulls the plough through the rows to flatten the earth around the century old vines.*
Behind her, the vineyard worker inhales the scents of the animal, mixed with the pungent chalk of the soil.

Hard to imagine that this arid land where even grass grows with difficulty, will enable this tiny one year old plant to mature, let alone be nourished for at least half a century!
.....and will produce grapes which will delight mankind well into the 21st century.

This downy bud snuggled on a vine shoot resembles a cocoon from which no butterfly will appear....., but the tender leaves form a circle around the promising manna.

At sunset in the Entre-deux-Mers, the alluvial soils are tinged with ochre and seem to dust themselves with talcum powder.
In the distance, a sanctuary tucked away in the countryside, one of the cooperative wine cellars of the Gironde, keeps watch over the latest harvests.

*𝒩o matter how one makes one's approach, one must still climb uphill to reach the romanesque church. This is to be expected, the village is called Montagne!
All around, undulating lands on a limestone plateau embrace the vineyards on wide terraces - a familiar landscape to the people of Saint Emilion.*

*Year after year, life begins again; the wonderful rebirth of the vegetative cycle.
At winter's end, bud break preceeds the opening up of tender, pastel tinted leaves
which begin to trap the first rays of sun. The vines flower gently, releasing subtle
and complex scents which only a walker through the vineyards in spring can reco-
gnize.
The vine, this ancient creeper resistant to the elements, firmly grasps with its tendrils
the wires which man has stretched out for it.*

A small corner of the vast region between the Dordogne and the Garonne rivers where man knows how to juxtapose vineyards with woody copses for other pleasures - these are the last refuges for much coveted game.

*W*hatever the season, whatever the task, these tireless workers appear to want to embrace the soil with their rounded backs so that it will yield its best fruits.

In the vicinity of Pauillac, to heighten the beauty of the landscape, man has had the wisdom to preserve a tree, to the detriment of a few vines.
.....They will be rewarded!

Evening falls and the ancient village of Fronsac bids goodnight to its vines, still touched by the sun on the slopes, and turns its gaze on the Dordogne which sprawls at its feet.

During good weather, heat is focused amongst the vineyard's rows.
The worker who staples the wires which she raises to enclose the generous leaves,
must be dreaming of the Atlantic beaches of the Médoc.
A winegrower stripping the leaves off a too vigourous vine and a worker flattening
the earth around the roots, chose the cool hours of the morning in which to carry
out their tasks.

𝒞lays, sands and gravels on slopes or on plateaux, the appellation of Lalande de Pomerol rejoices in a great diversity of soils where the Merlot grape grows magnificently.

RETOUR AUX SOURCES

Mets du sel gris dans ton bouillon,
Du sucre roux dans ta tisane
Et tu reprendras le sillon
Presque effacé par les savanes.

Dans le souffle d'éternité
Tu trouveras l'odeur des roses
Perdue au creux de la cité
Au bénéfice des névroses.

Le dialecte des animaux,
Des minéraux et des feuillages
Sera pour toi tissé de mots
Tout aussi simples qu'une image.

Retrouve autour d'un feu de bois
Les lutins de ton ascendance
Qui t'amèneront autrefois
Pour te conter des confidences.

Sache voir dans un reflet d'eau
Bien au-delà de la physique
Quelque clin d'oeil ou le cadeau
Fait par le jour à ta mystique.

Peut-être redeviendras-tu
L'homme qui fut mis sur la Terre
Pour en apprécier les vertus
Au lieu de les vendre aux enchères.

(Extrait de "Plaidoyer pour un Poète")
Poème de Denis REJANE

*I*n the Côtes de Bourg, on a vineyard's slope overhanging the estuary, a dovecote dating from the 15th century and disfigured with age, acts as a watchtower.

$\mathcal{V}$ineyards are planted on the higher ground, their roots kept dry, leaving the meadows rolling in hay to flirt with the Gironde as witnessed here in Saint Julien.

So many secret alcoves and bushes are concealed in our landscapes.....
Which wine hides behind this little cellar window, covered with wisteria?
At the end of a hot afternoon, why has a pretty young winegrower discarded her straw hat?

$\mathcal{T}$he rolling countryside of the Premières Côtes de Bordeaux which shelters in one of its folds, the old town of Langoiran, close to the Garonne river. During the winter, vinegrowers and fishermen unite over a large cooking pot where the marriage between wine and lampreys is consummated.

*F*ragile white grapes be they sauvignon, semillon or muscadelle do not suffer being squashed or crushed.

The hand of the harvester must be skilled to pick and place them with care in the baskets and fill up the crates.

Thus they arrive intact at the press from which a juice of great purity will be released.

𝒩ear Cussac-Fort-Médoc, the vines form a vast carpet of green where several paths or secluded alleys intersect to create different parcels.
Only the winegrower knows the secrets of their names and the quality of their soils.

This gravel soil intuitively knows how to filter and absorb excess water to the depths of the vine's roots and then how to replenish the plant in times of drought.

Thanks to these pebbles smoothed by a bygone eras and long travelled distances, the gravel stores the heat of the day and at night returns it to the already ripened grapes which sleep close by.

On the Côtes de Bourg, an old cellar hewn out of the limestone rock lies ready to protect the new born wine.

The damp and mushroomy aromas are stilled by the carbonic odours of fermentation which penetrate deep into the courtyard.

The widowed piles of stalks, stripped of their berries will become compost. The earth which grew them is waiting to be nourished by their lingering goodness.

Finally the long awaited harvest arrives!

Carefully placed at the trunk of the vine, a wooden basket becomes a temporary cradle.

*T*he clocktower of Saint Emilion tolls goodbye as the new harvest is amassed and packed into cases.
Swollen by the sun and covered by a light dust, the grapes are dressed in satiny cloaks.
They invite us to finger and crunch them for one last time before they disappear into the gaping mouth of the crusher-destemmer.

Merlot, Cabernet Sauvignon, Cabernet Franc and more seldom, Petit Verdot and Malbec, once ripened take on a velvety sheen with a host of ambiguous colours.
Are they black, red or blue?
During the harvest they are carried in baskets slung on the backs of pickers into trailer loads and arrive intact at the winery where expert hands are awaiting them, hovering over the selection table.
The unworthy berries are discarded.

A backdrop of green lushness for a harvest scene in the Graves where the actors are off-stage for the moment.

Symphony in red Bordeaux around an old vertical press where the wooden cage slowly allows the coloured tears to fall.
The pomace dries out slowly and once exhausted allows itself to be turned out like an enormous cake.
The mat of hemp, stained for life, must dry in the sun and await the next harvest.

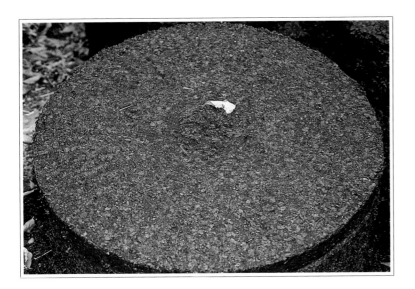

$\mathcal{T}$he Romans dug out the first furrows from the limestone rock to plant vines in the heart of the Saint Emilion plateau. Later, the medieval city spread out its vineyards on the neighbouring slopes and protected them within thick walls of stone, forming the famous "clos."

Who would have thought that at the end of the day, this little river, the Ciron, would take on magical powers. In becoming a snake of fog, it abandons its river bed and licks around the celebrated vineyards of Sauternes.

$\mathcal{T}$hese famous mists climb the gentle slopes around Preignac, Barsac and Sauternes, coating the golden fruit with their damp pearls and giving birth to their final travelling companion, the noble rot.

A wonderful freak of nature - the unexpected marriage between a grape and a mushroom which provokes botrytis. It makes itself at home in berry after berry creating the noble rot.
What a curious sight to see this harvest produced from successive pickings forming a mass of wrinkled and dusty browns from which will flow a delicate and subtle nectar, already rich with promising perfumes.

$\mathcal{A}$n indefinite time separates the moment when one bottles the young sweet wines with its clothes of light and the long awaited moment when one uncorks the wine enabling it to flow freely into the glass. Over the decades, this rich, unctuous liquid has taken on tones of amber and old gold.
Ssh! Our taste buds are getting impatient, let's drink.....

If Colbert had known that his oak trees in the forest of Troncais would end their lives by aging our great wines, would he be annoyed?
Without a doubt, he would want to taste them if he visited our cellars.

*W*ith time, the wine is clarified slowly in rows of oak barrels.
To separate it from its lees, the racking process enters the stage with an unusual set of props: Copper tap, hammer, wench, basin, glass and a watering can for topping up the barrels.
During the second winter, the wine is fined with egg whites, depositing the richest, pearly lees like fine moiré silk into a gleaming stainless steel basin.

On the Côtes de Castillon, the English and French crossed swords at the end of the 100 Years War.
Today, their descendants join forces to drink a toast to the glory of wine.

Soon the over abundant rains will glide joyfully over the limestone slopes of the Lussac Saint Emilion hills.
For the moment, the vines gently slumber under a sheltering sky, resting after the tumult of the harvest.

A traditional place, the barrel cellar gives personality to each chateau. *Occasionally it appears like a theatre set for a mime show.*

*I*n the belly of the barrels, the wine matures peacefully from month to month. Only one moment disturbs this long passage: the racking - a most delicate and crucial step in winemaking.

Every three months,the wine frees itself from the confines of the barrel, by way of a copper tap, in order to fill its lungs. It is the eye and the hand of the cellar master who with the aid of a light source, gently separates the deposits from the limpid wine.

A flickering flame, the smell of burning wax and the spiraling smoke of the candle have disappeared; today they have been replaced by an electric bulb which brightly lights the cellar master's glass.

In a Médoc vat room: the happy nuptials take place between wood and stainless steel. Carefully created gleaming modern vats with their conical bodies and rings for the thermal exchange of heat recall the old wooden vats held together by steel bands.
Planks and beams dance to the changing light of day, bringing to the smooth metal structures, the coarse grained warmth of wood.

*W*aiting *for the first cold spells, the leaves, stripped of their fruit, cling to the vines.*
They are dressed in their golden cloaks and imitate the colour of the new wine which will be born.

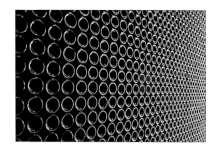

*W*ood, concrete or stainless steel, depending on the winemaker's choice, the vats are filled each year with white or red juice so that their vinification can begin.
One can listen to the noise, surprising in its intensity, of the bubbling of the must in the midst of fermentation.
Carried by pungent carbonic gases, one can smell the varying aromas of fruits and flowers which occasionally recall the slow jam-making of our grandmothers.

A wonderful showcase for the riches of the sea which beckon us to the feast. On the side, a glass awaits its moment of glory. The white wine of Bordeaux with its discrete charm but full of a myriad of subtle flavours will soon embellish the succulent dishes.

*W*hether one is for or against decanting wine, when sediment has formed, one should get rid of it.
So, let the ritual begin.....

 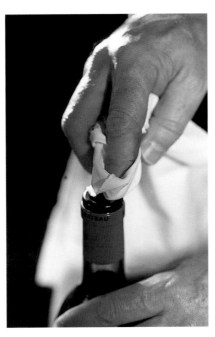  

The table has been set; in the dining room, the long necked decanters and expectant glasses have been gently filled with wine....all that is missing are the guests. Only the sun is allowed to enter, shedding its golden rays into the heart of every feast.

*G*rasp the glass firmly by its base and witness its gently swirling appearance.
*E*xperience the aromas evoking places that only one's memory can recall.
Finally touch the rim of crystal to one's lips bringing the desired wave of wine to the palate......this is the true pleasure of drinking.

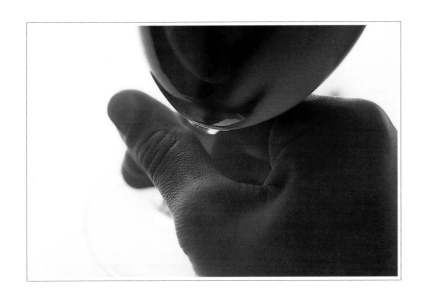

The grand ceremony of wine, simple or decorous, with long stemmed glasses or goblets, it hardly matters. Pleasure lights up the faces around the table when the wine is good.

THANK YOU ...

*This book was published with the support of
le CONSEIL REGIONAL d'AQUITAINE,
la MAIRIE de BORDEAUX,
le CONSEIL INTERPROFESSIONNEL du VIN de BORDEAUX,
le SYNDICAT VITICOLE de SAINT-EMILION*

Monsieur Olivier BERNARD - DOMAINE de CHEVALIER in LEOGNAN

OTHER THANKS TO THE WINERIES AND VATHOUSES' OWNERS

*p. 4 Stained-glassed window in the winery of château La Croix - Pomerol
p. 6 the old vathouse - château l'Angélus - Saint-Emilion
p. 91 the winery - château Saint-Robert - Pujols-sur-Ciron
p. 99 The winery - château Haut-Macô - Tauriac
p. 103 The vathouse - château Palmer - Margaux
p. 107 The vathouse - château Poujeaux - Moulis*

MORE GRATEFUL THANKS TO

*Monsieur Firmin Arambide (left) and Monsieur Michel Guérard (right) p. 109
Madame Corinne Guisez, château Faugères' owner - Saint-Emilion p. 113
and Mademoiselle Elise Fautré for her patience and beauty p. 115*

Published by

Editions Premiers Pas
58 bis avenue Charles De Gaulle - CLAOUEY - 33950 - LEGE-CAP-FERRET - FRANCE

Conception : Gilles d'AUZAC DE LA LAMARTINIE
Mise en pages : Francis CARNOY

Printed by : Imprimerie Balauze & Marcombe - 33610 CANÉJAN (FRANCE)

ISBN : 2 - 9509437 - 1 - 3

No part of this book may be reproduced, stored in a retrieval system or retransmited,
in any form or by any means, without the prior permission of the publishers.